# Mysterious MAGNETS

By Anastasia Suen

CELEBRATION PRESS
Pearson Learning

# Contents

**What Are Magnets?** . . . . . . . . . . . . . **3**

**Magnets and Compasses** . . . . . . . **6**

**One Giant Magnet!** . . . . . . . . . . . . **9**

**Magnetic Force** . . . . . . . . . . . . . . **14**

**Magnets, Electricity, Motors,
 and More!** . . . . . . . . . . . . . . . . . . **18**

**Glossary** . . . . . . . . . . . . . . . . . . . . **24**

**Index** . . . . . . . . . **Inside Back Cover**

# What Are Magnets?

For thousands of years, **magnets** have been a mystery. Long ago in Greece and China, people first discovered stones called **lodestones**. These stones were the first magnets. They attracted, or pulled, other objects toward them. Some metal objects even stuck to the stones. Early people thought they were magical!

How magnets work may seem like a mystery at first.

Lodestone is a hard, black, magnetic rock.

Lodestones are also called magnetite. Notice the smaller word *magnet* inside the word *magnetite*.

Magnets are made of metal. Everything that sticks to a magnet is also made of metal. Some metals, such as iron, steel, and nickel, stick to magnets. Other metals, such as aluminum, do not stick at all!

**Experiment**

## Magnetic, or Not?

You can test objects yourself to see whether they are magnetic.

1. Gather a group of objects from your classroom like the ones in the picture.
2. Test each object. Place a magnet over each object and try to lift it.

Does the magnet lift the object? If it does, the object is magnetic. If it doesn't, it's not magnetic.

5

# Magnets and Compasses

An ancient Chinese legend tells about Emperor Hwang-ti, who lived over 4,500 years ago. A thick fog surrounded the emperor during a battle. A figure attached to his chariot helped him out of the fog. The figure had an outstretched arm. The arm always pointed south because it had a lodestone inside.

We don't know whether this legend is true. However, we do know that the Chinese made the first **compasses** using lodestones. They discovered that one end of a lodestone pointed north. The other end pointed south. They used lodestones to help them find the four directions. These directions are north, south, east, and west.

The ancient Chinese once used a spoon-shaped compass like this one.

   Later, the Chinese learned how to make needles magnetic. They rubbed lodestones on sewing needles. Then they used the needles in their compasses.

   For hundreds of years, magnetic compasses have been important. They have helped sailors, explorers, and hikers find their way.

### Experiment

## Make a Water Compass

You can make a compass similar to one that the Chinese used.

1. Rub a magnet on a sewing needle. Rub the magnet **in the same direction** 30 times.
2. Tape the needle on a small piece of balsa wood, cork, or plastic.
3. Fill a plastic bowl with water. Place the magnetized needle into the bowl. The needle will point both north and south.

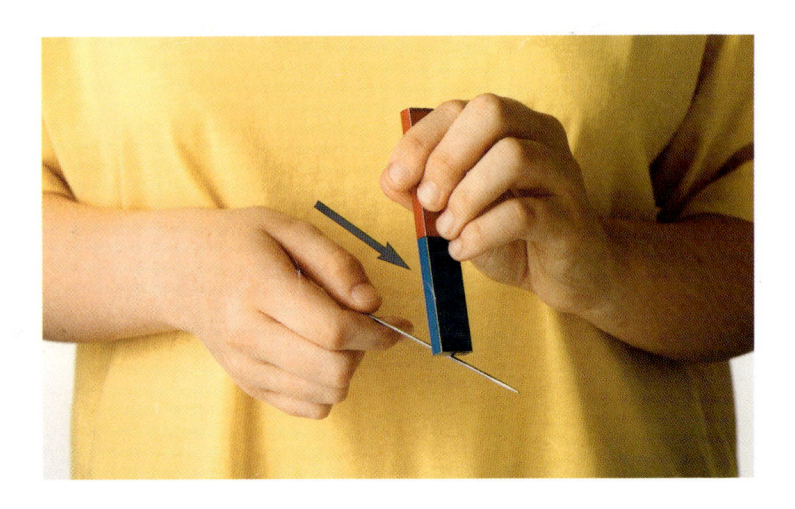

# One Giant Magnet!

People have tried many experiments with magnets. They have discovered some very interesting things. For example, if a magnet breaks, it does not lose its power. Pierre de Maricourt, a French engineer, discovered this in 1269. Each time he broke a magnet, one end became "north." The other end became "south." De Maricourt was the first person to write about the idea of magnetic **poles**.

The two ends of a magnet are called poles. Every magnet has a north pole and a south pole. Can you think of something else that has both a north and a south pole? If you guessed our planet Earth, you are right! In fact, Earth is a giant magnet! Try the experiment on the next page to see how magnetic poles affect each other.

# Experiment

## Poles Apart

The power of a magnet is strongest at the poles. Yet the poles do not always work together!

Place the poles of two magnets near each other. If the magnets grab each other, then a south pole is facing a north pole. If the magnets push each other away, then the poles are the same. South will push away south. North will push away north. They **repel** each other.

10

**North Pole**

**South Pole**

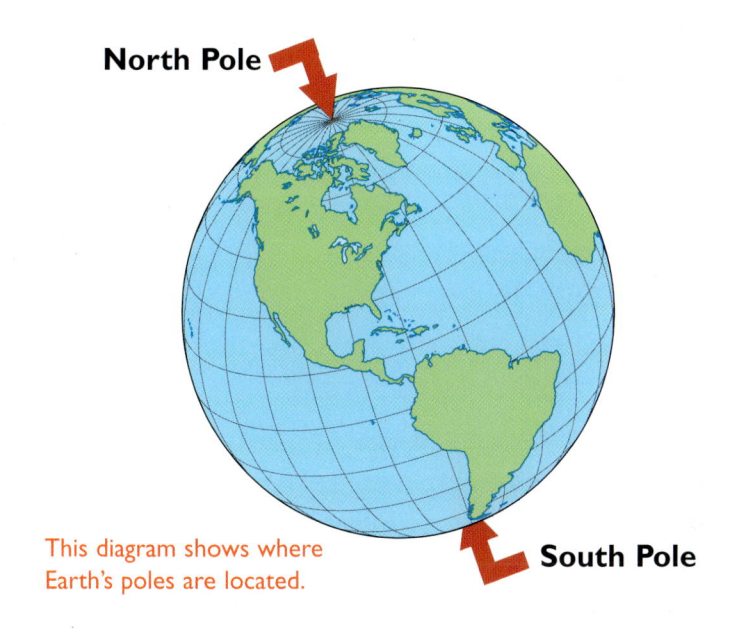

This diagram shows where Earth's poles are located.

Around 1600, William Gilbert, an English doctor, tested magnets. He put a lodestone into a small globe. Then he placed the small globe near a magnetic needle. The needle pointed to the north pole of the globe. Each time he placed the needle near the globe, it pointed north. Try the next experiment. See if you get the same results.

# Experiment

## Spinning Magnet

You can test Earth's magnetism as Gilbert did.

1. Loop a long string around a bar magnet. Tie a knot.
2. Stand up and hold the string so that the magnet hangs in the air. Gently spin the magnet. Wait until the magnet stops. Which way does the magnet point?
3. Use a compass to find the direction.
4. Try the test one more time.

Did the compass needle point toward the north each time? All magnets point to Earth's **magnetic north pole**. The magnetic north pole is different from the **geographic North Pole**.

Earth's geographic North Pole is in the Arctic Circle. It is always in the same place. The magnetic north pole, called Mag North, doesn't stay in the same place. As Earth spins, the iron in its core moves. This movement changes where Mag North is located. It is now in Canada, about 1,200 miles from the geographic North Pole.

It may seem as if a compass doesn't work on Earth's magnetic north pole. Because the location is already on magnetic north, the magnet inside just spins or dips down. So it doesn't look as if the needle is "pointing" anywhere.

# Magnetic Force

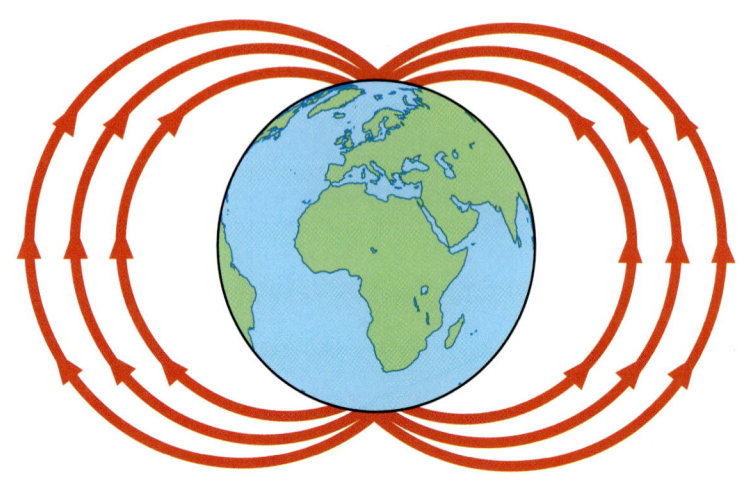

Like other magnets, Earth also has a magnetic field.

The **magnetic field** around every magnet is invisible, but it is very powerful. Some animals, such as birds, whales, dolphins, and snails, have a built-in magnet. As a result, they can feel Earth's magnetic field. Scientists think that the magnet acts like a compass to help them find their way when they travel. No one really knows how.

**Experiment**

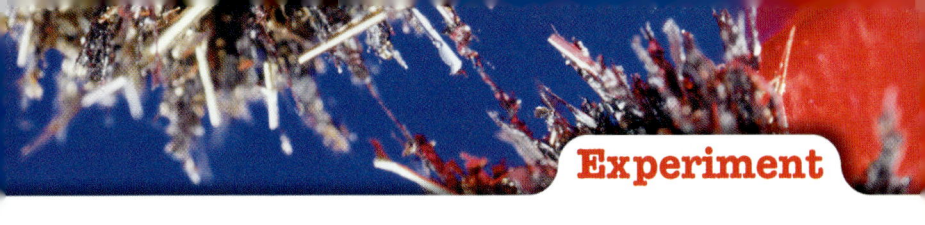

## Test Magnetic Force

You can test the force of a magnet's magnetic field. You will need a piece of paper or cardboard, a bar magnet, and iron filings. Iron filings are tiny pieces of iron. You can get them at a hobby store, or ask an adult to make some by filing an iron nail.

1. Sprinkle iron filings on the paper or cardboard.
2. Put the magnet under the paper.
3. Lightly tap the paper.
4. What happens to the filings?

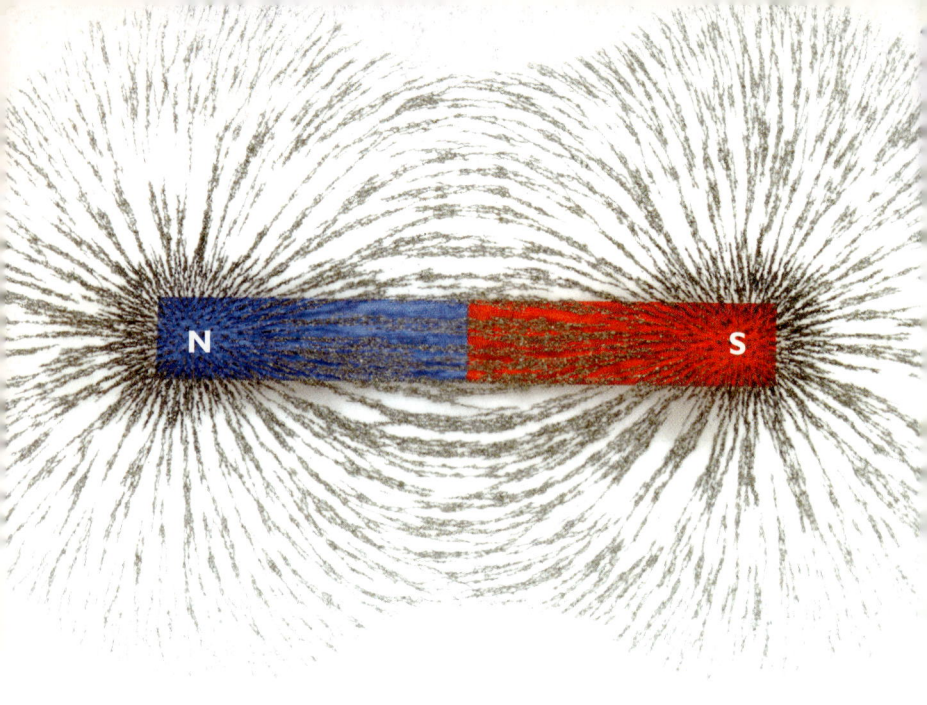

Iron filings form patterns that show the lines of force.

As you can see from the experiment on page 15, the magnet moves the filings into curved lines. These lines are called **lines of force**. They show you the magnetic field around the magnet. They also show you that though the magnet's force works all around it, the magnet is strongest at its poles.

**Experiment**

# Making Magnets

Magnets are powerful! Try this to test the power of a magnet.

1. Touch a paper clip with a magnet. Lift the magnet so the paper clip hangs down.

2. Now touch another paper clip with the first paper clip. The magnet has magnetized the paper clip. Next, touch a third and then a fourth paper clip. How many paper clips can your magnet hold?

# Magnets, Electricity, Motors, and More!

Electricity is all around you. You use it every day. With just the flick of a switch or the press of a button you can turn on a light. You can use televisions, stereos, and computers because of electricity.

Electricity is caused by tiny particles called **electrons**. Electrons move easily through metal. Their flow is called an electric current.

What do electrons and electricity have to do with magnets? Electricity and magnets have a lot to do with each other.

In 1820 in Denmark, a science professor named Hans Christian Oersted made an amazing discovery. His discovery showed something very important about magnetism.

These generators create power for the lighthouse.

Oersted was doing experiments with his class. He placed a compass near a piece of wire. The wire had electricity running through it. The compass needle moved! This showed that an electric current could create a magnetic field.

In 1831, English scientist Michael Faraday made the first electric **generator**. He created an electric current using a horseshoe magnet and wires.

Besides electricity, magnetism is used in many other ways. Some magnets in your home are easy to see. You may use magnets to clip notes to your refrigerator. A magnet also holds the can lid when you open a can of food with an electric can opener.

The chart below shows just a few of the things that have magnets in them. It also explains how magnets work in each item.

| Everyday Magnets | |
|---|---|
| **Doorbell** | Electric current flows through magnetic field around magnet in center of doorbell, which produces doorbell sound. |
| **Refrigerator** | Weak magnets hold door tightly closed. |
| **Credit Card** | Stripe on the back is made up of tiny bar magnets with coded information. |
| **Conveyor Belt** | Magnets hold and transport iron and steel cans. |
| **Train** | Strong magnets in some trains now being developed enable them to float over tracks to reduce **friction**. |
| **Subway Ticket Machine** | Magnets help sort coins into different values. |

As you can see from the chart on page 20, some items, such as a refrigerator or a credit card, have magnets that are used in simple ways. Other things use magnets in more complicated ways.

The sounds and pictures in audio- and videotapes are recorded with magnets. Magnets in computer disks are used to store and copy information. Telephones, microwave ovens, dishwashers, and cars also use magnets.

Sometimes magnets are used in places such as airports or amusement parks. Many of these places have large metal detectors that people must walk through. A metal detector, which is like a large archway, has powerful magnets inside of it. The magnets detect, or identify, anything made of metal, such as coins, keys, or jewelry.

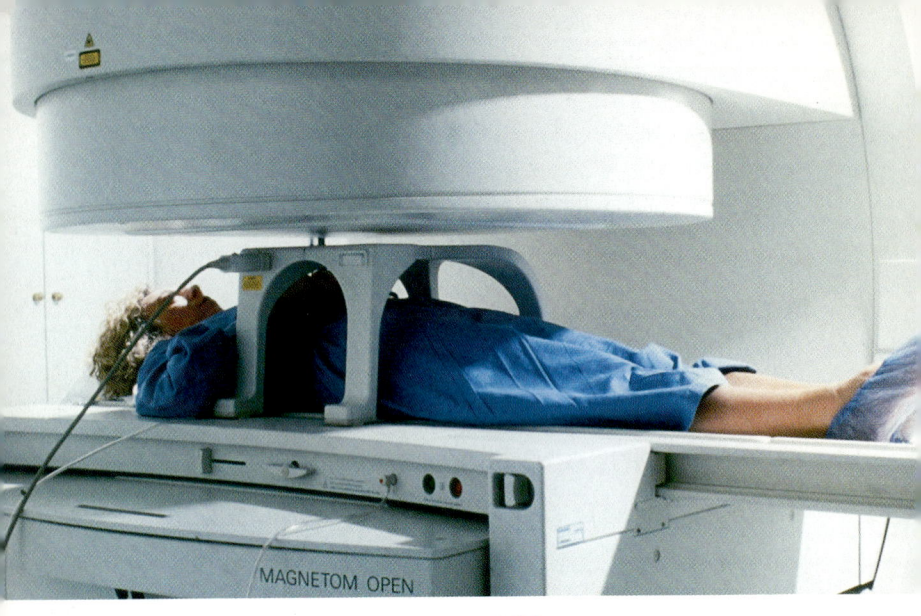

This patient is getting an MRI examination.

Magnets are also used in medicine. An MRI (magnetic resonance imaging) scanner uses magnets to see inside the human body. Some atoms in the body have magnetic characteristics. The scanner combines the magnetic field around the body with radio waves. This creates an image similar to an X-ray. Using this machine, doctors often can find out what is wrong with their patients without having to perform surgery.

Now that you've learned many interesting facts about magnets, here are two fun activities for you to try.

### Amazing Plastic Plate Art

1. Tape a magnet to the top (serving side) of a plastic plate. Turn the plate over.
2. Scatter paper clips or other small metal objects over the plate. **Do not use any sharp or pointed iron shapes!**
3. Use your fingers to pull the paper clips or other objects into different shapes.

### The Flying Butterfly

1. Cut a butterfly shape out of tissue paper.
2. Tie one end of a thread (about 2 feet long) to a paper clip.
3. Tape the paper clip onto the top of the butterfly. Then tape the other end of the thread to a tabletop.
4. Hold a magnet over the paper clip. Do you think you can make the butterfly fly?

# Glossary

| | |
|---|---|
| **compasses** | instruments used for showing direction |
| **electrons** | very small, invisible particles that move outside the nucleus of an atom |
| **friction** | the force that slows the motion of two surfaces that touch each other |
| **generator** | a machine that uses magnets to create an electric current |
| **geographic North Pole** | located in the Arctic Circle; where Earth spins |
| **lines of force** | lines that form around a magnet |
| **lodestones** | rocks that are naturally magnetic |
| **magnets** | objects that pull other objects toward themselves |
| **magnetic field** | the space around a magnet where the magnet has power |
| **magnetic north pole** | a compass needle points to the magnetic north pole |
| **poles** | the two ends of a magnet |
| **repel** | to push away |